This book is to be returned on or before the last date stamped below

780.9

FIFE REGIONAL EDUCATION LIBRARY

FIFE EDUCATIONAL RESOURCES CENTRE
RAMSAY ROAD KIRKCALDY

Ludwig van Beethoven

by Pam Brown

OTHER TITLES IN THE SERIES
John Lennon by Michael White (1-85015-304-3)
Wolfgang Amadeus Mozart by Michael White
    (1-85015-300-0)
Peter Ilyich Tchaikovsky by Michael Pollard
    (1-85015-303-5)
Antonio Vivaldi by Pam Brown (1-85015-301-9)
Coming Soon
Johann Sebastian Bach (1-85015-311-6)
Frédéric Chopin by Pam Brown (1-85015-310-8)
Elton John (1-85015-369-8)
Bob Marley by Marsha Bronson (1-85015-312-4)
Sting by Marsha Bronson (1-85015-368-X)

Picture Credits:
Front Cover, AKG at Image Select; AKG at Image Select; Bildarchiv Ost
Nationalbibliothek; Bridgeman Art Library; Marshall Cavendish; Mary Evans;
Picturepoint; Reed Consumer Books; Roger-Viollet; Spectrum; Telegraph Colour
Library; Zefa.

Published in Great Britain in 1993
by Exley Publications Ltd,
16 Chalk Hill, Watford,
Herts WD1 4BN, United Kingdom.

A copy of the CIP data is available from the
British Library on request.

ISBN 1-85015-302-7

Series editor: Helen Exley
Editor: Samantha Armstrong
Picture research: Alex Goldberg/James Clift
of Image Select
Editing: Margaret Montgomery
Glossary and Recommended Listening, Music
and Education Advisor: Jill Simms
Typeset by Delta
Watford, UK
Printed and bound in Hungary.

Ludwig van
BEETHOVEN

by Pam Brown

Prelude

The setting was magnificent – glowing with silks and velvets, bright with gilding and glittering chandeliers. The audience was elegantly dressed, the ladies' jewels were throwing off sparkles of light. But no one had eyes for their surroundings. All were caught up in sound – in music that overwhelmed all other senses; music that spoke to their minds and hearts as perhaps no music had ever done before. It spoke of the restlessness of the human spirit and its struggle to endure through terror and despair. But now, in this last movement, all doubt and fear seemed to give way to a great shout of joy and exultation.

Whatever we suffer, the music seemed to cry, it is wonderful to be alive. To glory in beauty, to see and hear, to love and to be loved, simply to exist, to be a part of life, is worth any price we have to pay. The orchestra had not been enough for the composer to express his vision – a great chorus of voices sang out the words of the poet Schiller's 'Ode To Joy".

As the last note died away, there was complete silence – and then an explosion of applause.

A stocky man with a shock of untidy hair stood facing the orchestra, unmoving. Then a young singer stepped forward and, taking him gently by the shoulders, turned him to face the audience.

He saw them rise, saw their applauding hands. But no sound of their acclamation penetrated the silence that surrounded him.

He was totally deaf.

Ludwig van Beethoven had given his last symphony to the world – his ninth, the *Choral* Symphony.

In our own time the final movement has been adopted as a symbol of friendship among nations – the expression of the hopes of men and women for a better future. Yet this great exultation of faith and joy came from the mind of a man sick in body, and deaf for half his lifetime.

A family of musicians

Ludwig van Beethoven was the son and grandson of musicians. His grandfather was a fine bass singer and a gifted musician. He was employed by the Elector of Cologne, who kept court at Bonn, a beautiful town set on the banks of the River Rhine. At that time Germany was made up of small states, ruled by Electors, who lived like royalty. Back in the Middle Ages, a group of princes had been chosen to elect the emperor of the country – and, as "Electors" in Beethoven's day, these princes had considerable power and presided over their own courts.

For their pleasure, and for the entertainment of important guests, the Electors established their own orchestras. These were extremely important in giving employment to the composers and the musicians of the day ... although, as employees, the musicians were often treated little better than servants.

Ludwig's grandfather was the *Kapellmeister,* or Master of the Chapel, a post of considerable dignity – though it was not very well paid.

Ludwig's father, Johann, was also employed at the court, as a singer and violinist, but despite his very real ability, luck seemed to pass him by and he was never a great success.

Parents

In 1767 Johann married a young widow named Maria. The newly-weds did not have much money and moved into rooms in the house of a family

The façade of Ludwig van Beethoven's birthplace in Bonn, Germany. It is now treated like a shrine although it was far shabbier when Beethoven was a boy. In Bonn, as in most cities, the rich and the poor lived together; Beethoven was to straddle both societies during his life.

named Fischer. Maria was a slight woman, pious and kindly. Her life had been scarred with tragedy; the death of her father, that of her first husband and, after her marriage to Johann, the death of her mother. She was always inclined to be very serious – the Fischers never recalled having seen her laugh.

Maria and Johann's first baby died, but less than two years later, on December 16, 1770, another son was born to them. They named him Ludwig, after the little boy they had lost – Ludwig van Beethoven.

Johann struggled to make a living, taking job after job – often doing far more work than he could manage. Time and again he applied for promotion or for an increase in salary but with no success. Maria gave birth to seven children and as the family grew, so did its poverty. Dispirited, Johann turned to drink. And Maria was becoming very ill. It was the quiet onset of the tuberculosis – a bacterial disease of the lungs – that could kill her if she did not get proper food and rest. She found it increasingly difficult to cope with her home and family.

A second Mozart

Ludwig van Beethoven was growing up surrounded by music, for although the family was poor, there were always visitors in the house – singers, actors, instrumentalists. And there was constant talk of music, concerts and touring.

There is no evidence that Ludwig was a natural prodigy, a child genius like Mozart or Handel. But his father set him to the study of music when he was very small indeed – perhaps only four years old.

Johann knew himself to be a failure, but in his little son he saw a gleam of hope. He remembered that Mozart had been paraded around Europe as a musical genius, astonishing all who heard him and being showered with money and gifts. In Johann's plan, Ludwig was to be turned into a second Mozart. He seemed determined to

Top: Ludwig's mother, Maria van Beethoven, was gentle and unassuming although prone to outbursts of temper as she grew older. Beethoven was close to his mother and grieved deeply at her death. Above: Ludwig's father, Johann van Beethoven, was a tenor at court. Jovial with companions but strict with his eldest son, he pushed Ludwig into music at the age of only about four years old.

Above: Beethoven's first harpsichord was probably not so fine as this one. The harpsichord was the forerunner of the piano. In a harpsichord the strings are plucked, whereas in a piano they are struck with hammers. Finger pressure makes no difference to the tone of a harpsichord and very little dynamic expression is possible whereas the piano can be played both loudly, forte, and quietly, piano.
Right: Beethoven's piano and violin in the Beethoven House museum. Beethoven's technique was very different from the traditional way of playing the harpsichord. He was often breaking the strings of the pianos he played!

make a musician out of Ludwig in order to gain the fame and wealth he himself had never known.

Every day Ludwig had his music lessons from his father and every day he was made to play, hour after hour. Passers-by would see the poor child at the clavier, sometimes weeping from weariness as he played.

Meanwhile, the games of childhood were few and far between, though Ludwig and his brothers would sometimes play with local children – the Beethoven contingent whooping and shouting with the rest. Ludwig loved to be carried piggyback, roaring with laughter as he was jolted about the yard. He had a happy and loving nature – a stocky, blunt-faced, dark-skinned boy full of determination. Because of his dark skin he was known as *Der Spagnol* – the Spaniard.

All his life Beethoven would explode into loud laughter when he was amused – sometimes at the most inappropriate times and places – and he was always to have a rather schoolboy sense of fun.

He was shabby and none too clean. Maria's illness meant that the children were left largely to the servants and showed every sign of their neglect. When Ludwig started school he was a sadly scruffy child. He was no scholar and his lack of achievement made his father all the more determined that he should make a life in music. He was taken away from school and made to concentrate all the harder on his musical studies. He became more and more isolated as Johann made him devote all his time to music practice.

Another child might have lost every scrap of enthusiasm under such pressure – but Ludwig found that the more he learned, the more he wanted to discover.

He was falling in love with music.

Before the advent of television and radio, families gathered together for the evening. In Beethoven's home, there was a lot of musical activity. Johann was teaching young Ludwig on the keyboard and other teachers would come and go from the house. Beethoven's younger brothers, Caspar Carl and Johann, did not have any of the musical ability that Ludwig was blessed with.

"But wasn't it beautiful?"

Johann could laugh among his friends – but when it came to his son's education there was little cheerfulness or understanding. Ludwig was absolutely forbidden to try things just for fun, whether at the keyboard, the violin or the viola. His father was furious if he found him playing without notes, making up little tunes. It was no good Ludwig saying, "But wasn't it beautiful?".

"You are not ready to play things out of your head," his father would say. "When you have become good enough, then you can...."

It was harsh – but the habit of self discipline in music was to stay with Ludwig all his life. Johann knew that without knowledge and technique a musician does not have the building blocks from which to build new things.

Performance

By the time Ludwig was seven his father had sufficient confidence in him to allow him to perform in public. Johann took him to play before the ladies and gentlemen of the court, and when this proved a great success, to the great city of Cologne.

Johann took two years off his son's age to make his skill seem all the more remarkable...a fact Ludwig was not to discover until he was forty.

Ludwig had soon outgrown his father's teaching and the search began for more knowledgeable instructors. One, Tobias Pfieffer, proved an excellent teacher – but enjoyed Johann's company at the tavern rather too much. The two men would roll home drunk, wake the nine-year-old boy, and set him to working at his music until late into the night.

By the time he was ten, Ludwig had gained a very good grounding in several instruments, but it was the sound of the organ that particularly enchanted him. With the self-confidence he had gained from his rather eccentric upbringing he took himself off to the local monastery and introduced himself to one of the friars, an

Christian Gottlob Neefe, the teacher who gave Beethoven the understanding he so desperately needed. Neefe was also the first to recognize the talent in the eleven-year-old and had Beethoven's first works published for him. Beethoven appreciated Neefe's influence saying, "If I ever become well-known, it will partly be your doing."

eminent organist who liked the boy's enthusiasm and took him on as his pupil. Ludwig made such extraordinary progress that soon Friar Willibald Koch made him his assistant. Even this was not enough for Ludwig. He sought out other organists and bigger organs. At ten he was far better than a fellow student who was twenty.

And he was composing. There is a story that the pieces that he was writing were too difficult for his small hands to cope with. "Why, you can't play that, Ludwig!" said his teacher. "I will when I am bigger," replied the boy.

Progress

As part of the Elector's entourage, Johann van Beethoven often had to accompany the Elector on his travels – but sometimes the Elector's business did not include musicians and they were free to do as they pleased. Johann used the time to take his son to give concerts in the great houses, the castles and the abbeys of the region. It opened Ludwig's eyes to the wider world, but he liked it best when he could be alone, engrossed in his own thoughts. Though he was still young, he no longer seemed a child. Music was becoming his life.

Johann recognized that it was time to find an exceptional teacher for the boy. Johann chose a man named Christian Gottlob Neefe, the new court organist. It was a turning point in Ludwig's life. Neefe was stern in his criticisms, but a most excellent teacher and a good friend to this young boy, so cut off from ordinary companionship.

In 1782 Neefe was obliged to travel with the Elector, and so had to leave someone to take over his duties while he was away from Bonn. He chose Ludwig, who was only eleven and a half.

To encourage the boy, Neefe had nine of Ludwig's variations on different musical themes for the piano printed. "This youthful genius is deserving of help to enable him to travel. He would surely become a second Wolfgang Amadeus Mozart were he to continue as he has

Archduke of Austria and Elector of Cologne, Maximillian Franz. In the days of the court, musicians were employed by the aristocracy. Maximillian loved music and his court was full of orchestras and chamber groups. Johann van Beethoven was in his employment and so was Ludwig. It was a great opportunity for the young boy to play with experienced musicians.

MAXIMILIANUS.
Archidux Austr; Ord. Teut; suprem.
Magister, Archiepiscop. Coloniens;
et Episcop: Monaster. Coadjutor.

begun," claimed Neefe.

Johann's dream for his eldest son was starting to come true.

> "I thank you for the counsel which you gave me so often in my progress in my divine art. If I ever become a great man yours shall be a share of the credit."
>
> Beethoven, in a letter to his teacher, Neefe.

Hopes

In Beethoven's day an orchestra was led not from the conductor's podium but from the harpsichord or pianoforte. From here the conductor guided the performance and directed from the musical score. Ludwig, at twelve years old, now began to deputize for the *Kapellmeister* in this position. He was paid nothing, as an apprentice, but the experience was invaluable. In the years to come he

was to astound people with his ability to read and play from the most difficult and intricate musical score at first sight. Then, in 1784, Ludwig was given a salaried post as assistant Court Organist and he began to give lessons to supplement that income.

The Beethoven family must have believed that at last their life was to be a little easier – but their elation was short-lived. Johann's voice, on which the family largely depended for its income, was failing. And Ludwig's mother, Maria, was becoming increasingly ill as the months went by.

It was vital that Ludwig, as the eldest son, find a better salaried post that would bring money into

This is the sort of concert at which the young Beethoven appeared, as the child Mozart and his sister had done before him. Educated people prided themselves on their musical ability and understanding, and the nobility would sometimes perform with the professional musicians they employed.

With the von Breuning family Beethoven moved away from the life he had been used to. He could now read and learn about the ancient literature of Greece and Rome, of sculpture and art.

the home. It seemed the survival of the family largely rested on his ability to find and hold a job. At fourteen his days of childhood were clearly over and the strains of this told on him for the rest of his life.

He was still known as *Der Spagnol,* "a boy powerfully, almost clumsily built" and radiating determination. He walked bent forward, full of purpose.

He needed determination. Johann was drinking more and more heavily and Maria's condition was deteriorating steadily. The court records note that Johann's voice was now "stale". Dismissal was in the air.

Ludwig himself was put down as being "of good ability, still young, of quiet and good disposition."

Both father and son were listed as "poor".

Opportunities

Living in Bonn at this time was a wealthy, generous, kind and very happy family – the von Breunings. They had taken a young medical student, Franz Wegeler, under their wing, and he in turn introduced them to his friend Ludwig van Beethoven.

Ludwig made a great impression on the family, both by his ability and his good heartedness, and they asked him to give music lessons to two of the children.

After having lived in poverty and with such a burden of responsibility, it was an unbelievable happiness for young Ludwig to be allowed to visit people in this educated and warmly-affectionate family. In the von Breuning home he found new joys and new interests.

All about him was talk of art and science and politics and he was introduced to the literature of ancient Greece and Rome – things of which he had previously known nothing. It was good to have a retreat from the pressures of his family. The von Breunings and Franz Wegeler were to remain his friends all his life.

Vienna

In the spring of 1787, Ludwig van Beethoven managed to raise enough money to travel to Vienna – a city where he knew he would find the best orchestras, the best performers and the best composers.

Mozart, aged thirty-one, was already established in Vienna. It was arranged that sixteen-year-old Ludwig play for him. At first Mozart seemed to give him only half his attention – and to regard his performance as merely an elaborately-prepared set piece. Irked, Beethoven asked Mozart to give him a theme for improvisation. Improvising was one of Beethoven's greatest gifts and his performance startled Mozart out of his apathy. When he had finished playing Mozart said to his friends "Keep your eyes on him; some day he will give the world something to talk about."

Mozart agreed to give Ludwig lessons but Beethoven was to later say that Mozart had "a fine but choppy way of playing." The manner

A silhouette of Beethoven and an "autograph" manuscript – handwritten by the composer – composed when he was just fifteen, as in the portrait.

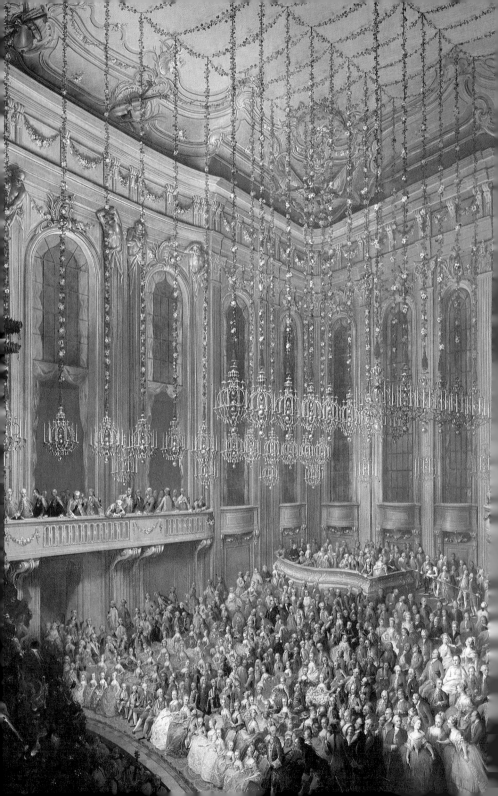

suited to the clavier and harpsichord was very different to that demanded by the developing pianoforte. The harpsichord had a mechanism whereby the string was plucked by a quill giving a light sound. Because the forte-piano, as it was initially known, used a hammer to hit the string it produced both loud (forte) and soft (piano) sounds and it could also sustain notes with the pedal, unlike the harpsichord. The piano was where Beethoven's interest lay.

The music written for the earlier instruments could, as with Bach and Mozart, be magnificent – some of the greatest music the world has ever known – but Beethoven was looking for a new technique that would give him greater attack, a richer sound, a wider range.

The young Beethoven delighted in the vivid cosmopolitan world of Vienna. The excitement of the city, independence, Mozart's praise – it all sang in his head. It seemed the world was opening up to him.

"Mozart's school: clear and markedly brilliant playing based more on staccato than legato; a witty and lively execution. The pedal is rarely used and never necessary. Beethoven's manner: characteristic and passionate strength, alternating with all the charms of smooth cantabile, is the outstanding feature."

Carl Czerny.

"... my best friend"

But his stay in Vienna was to last only two weeks. A letter came from his father. His mother was dying. Ludwig rushed home. He wrote that he "found his mother still alive, but in a deplorable state". The tuberculosis that had made her life so hard for so long had at last overcome her.

Beethoven was with her for those last weeks. When she died, he wrote simply, "She was such a kind, loving mother to me, and my best friend."

Probably because of his distress, Ludwig had a bad attack of what he believed at the time to be asthma, and was haunted by the fact that he might have tuberculosis like his mother. He complained to a friend, "To this is added melancholy, almost as great as my malady itself." This is the first record of the terrible depressions that were to overcome him at intervals throughout his life.

The family was now left with very little money. Ludwig had spent all he had on his visit to Vienna – and Johann all his savings in caring for Maria.

Opposite: The wealth of court life is shown in this picture of a theatrical performance; the elaborate costumes, the decorations and the myriad of candles create a glittering and gorgeous scene. Beethoven moved successfully into aristocratic circles. His first piano performances were in the palaces and homes of the high society.

17

It was a sad and desperate household.

Then yet another blow fell. Just four months later, Ludwig's dearly loved seven-month-old sister, Margaret, died.

Ludwig was still only in his seventeenth year, but had the cares of a grown man. There seemed nowhere to turn. The year that had begun so joyfully for him was ending in despair.

Head of the family

Of the seven children born to Johann and Maria only three were now still alive – Ludwig, Casper Carl and young Johann. The loss of Maria had hit Ludwig's father, Johann, hard. Once he had been a lighthearted drunk – now he drank from despair. The boys stood by him, fetching him from the town when he was helplessly drunk and, on occasion, persuading the police to let them take him home, rather than locking him up.

Left: Bonn, the pleasant town beside the Rhine where Beethoven grew up. He loved to explore the city and the countryside that lay beyond it. But Bonn could not give Beethoven the musical experience he knew he needed and he realized he would have to leave very quickly.

Left: A concert for the flute and keyboard held in a palace. This is the kind of musical gathering that the Elector, Maximillian, would have held at the court in Bonn and which Beethoven would have been familiar with before he went to Vienna.

And money became an increasing problem. A petition to the Elector gave Johann, now dismissed from his post, a small pension. A little of the money was to be paid to him, so long as he kept out of trouble. The rest was put in the safe keeping of Ludwig who, sensitively, made some of the money over to his humiliated father.

Mercifully, at this point Ludwig was at long last given a properly paid position at court.

He was made one of the viola players in the new court *Theater* in Bonn and was given the post of Chamber Musician. His name as an organist still appeared in the court listings, but he had a place both in the chapel and *Theater* orchestras.

The orchestra

It was in the next four years, working with the orchestra and playing a wide range of music, that Beethoven gained new and vital experience. His career coincided with great changes in orchestras.

Up to the end of the seventeenth century, ensembles had been very varied in their make up. It was not until the eighteenth century that instruments settled down into accepted groups – for instance, the four-part string quartet. It was in the eighteenth century, too, that the woodwind section became standardized – with two each of flutes, oboes, clarinets and bassoons. In time more have been added. Violin-making also reached an incredible degree of perfection. And when trumpets and horns acquired valves it was a great step forward.

Earlier instruments were sometimes thin in sound and at times appallingly unreliable, particularly those of the woodwind. Until instruments became dependable in performance and developed greater flexibility and range, the modern orchestra could not evolve, and the structure of a musical composition could not have the weight or complexity that was later possible.

The development of the court orchestra was very important in the story of music. It was the orchestra of the Elector of Mannheim that did most to change the form of the orchestra and make the symphony (composed for the full orchestra) possible. In the mid-eighteenth century the Mannheim Orchestra mastered the playing of controlled diminuendi, becoming softer, and crescendi, becoming louder, and it explored new possibilities in technique.

The orchestra in which Beethoven was working compared well with that of Mannheim and he learned a great deal about the capabilities of instruments and the possibilities of using instruments in imaginative ways.

Influential friends

When the orchestra was in Bonn, Beethoven spent a lot of time with the von Breunings – and it was probably in their house that he met Count Ferdinand Waldstein, a great friend of the Elector and a man of some influence. The Count was one of the first to foresee the greatness that lay ahead for the young musician and he helped Beethoven by giving him gifts of money and a grand piano.

Beethoven toured a great deal with the orchestra and had the chance to hear master musicians. As a result he changed his old manner of playing the piano. This was made possible by the dramatic changes in piano construction, changes which gave the instrument a new richness and range. He was also thinking of new ways of writing music and was becoming more and more deeply involved in composition.

When the Elector was away, Beethoven would use his freedom to walk in the countryside around Bonn, caught up in his music. His ideas came to him in the quietness and beauty of the hills and meadows and woods. A bird or the song of a stream could inspire him, and he would capture the moment in the notebooks he always carried.

Music was not his only delight. He was beginning to fall in love, usually with his pupils. His friends were inclined to believe that he was *always* in love! But when it came to a choice

The making of a violin. For two hundred·years the finest violins were made in Italy by the Amati, Guarneri and Stradivari families. The form of the instrument has remained almost unchanged for four hundred years, although thinner strings and a higher bridge appeared in the nineteenth century. The present bow (concave) replaced the old form (convex) in the nineteenth century. When instruments began to be made in a certain style with a fixed sound, the development of the larger orchestras became possible. Beethoven used a whole range of instruments in his compositions.

between love and music – music always won.

Beethoven gave his whole heart and mind to his work and was always looking for opportunities to learn and improve. At the age of twenty-two, he was offered a wonderful chance. One of the greatest and most prolific composers of his day, Haydn, had visited Bonn and been very impressed by some compositions young Beethoven had given him. Now the Elector – probably persuaded by Count Waldstein – gave Beethoven leave of absence and money enough to go back to Vienna and study under Haydn. The Elector expected Beethoven to come back and give the court the benefit of any new skills that he had acquired. But when, on November 2, 1792, Beethoven left Bonn for Vienna it was for good. He was never to go back.

He lost no time in adjusting to his new life in Vienna – a city that seemed the very heart of Europe, beautiful and brilliant, a magnet for the gifted and famous. The stocky, scruffy, plain young man bought new clothes, taking great care to note what he spent his money on, and even

Vienna, Beethoven's destination when he left Bonn aged twenty-two. Vienna welcomed him with open arms: the nobility praised, supported and encouraged him despite his strange moods. Beethoven himself said he always wanted to leave Vienna and was only kept there by circumstances. He would leave in the summer for the countryside and return to the town refreshed and rested.

ook dancing lessons, though he was never to be a uccess on the ballroom floor.

However, soon after his arrival a letter reached im telling him that his father was dead. It was a ad but also worrying time, for it seemed likely hat the pension that supported his sons would ie with him. Beethoven hastily wrote to the Elector and was relieved to hear that not only ould it continue, but that the amount would be oubled. The Elector, of course, still expected his rotégé to return to Bonn.

The composition lessons with Haydn began and Beethoven was also making formidable progress s a pianist. However, although Haydn thought ighly of his student, Beethoven was disap- ointed with Haydn's methods.

To improve his composition Beethoven still esperately needed a sound knowledge of techni- alities, especially counterpoint, the combining f two or more melodies together.

He knew he had to work incredibly hard if he as to achieve his musical ambition. Composi- on never came easily. The ideas in his head had

Above: The Esterhazy Palace, one of the homes of Prince Nicolaus Esterhazy. Beethoven was supported financially by various nobles, but he broke away from the patronage system. He was often a guest of the aristocracy – normally to compose or teach while he was there.

to be harnessed with tremendous concentration – and were the result of years of intense study and much trial and error. He rarely borrowed ideas from other composers, as many of his contemporaries did – but he frequently reworked themes he had used before, in his own compositions, expanding and clarifying them. His notebooks are a mass of corrections and he wrote with such speed and enthusiasm that they are often very difficult to decipher.

He was introduced to a teacher named Johann Schenk who wanted to give this young man the help he needed, but without offending Haydn. He only agreed to teach Beethoven if he was not paid and the lessons were kept secret. Under Schenk's guidance Beethoven learned fast and well. Haydn was delighted – for Schenk insisted that all the corrections he made were rewritten in Beethoven's own handwriting.

Unfortunately, Haydn sent examples of his pupil's "new" work to the Elector back in Bonn – only to be told that they had been written before Beethoven had left. This led to a coolness between teacher and pupil – though the old master and the new always respected each other's work. The affair may have been merely a misunderstanding – but Beethoven could be very devious at times.

It was now that Beethoven turned to a great musical theorist, Albrechtsberger, for more advanced tuition. The man was a disciplinarian and worked Beethoven to his limits, but Beethoven knew it was the price he must pay if he was to achieve anything worthwhile. He could not express what was in his head if he did not have the knowledge and techniques to enable him to get it on to paper and so to performance.

A difficult man

While Beethoven studied he gave concerts in wealthy homes – and his reputation grew steadily. Vienna had few public concerts at that time but the nobility held concerts in their homes. Prince

Vienna was an exciting city, the streets noisy with the sound of hoofs and carriage wheels, and busy with people from every walk of life. The cafés and inns were loud with conversation and laughter – and society revelled in concerts and balls. Beethoven was well-known in the city as he looked so distinctive. His manners were also unusual – he was known to walk out of a restaurant without paying, but the owner simply put it down to artistic temperament.

Karl Lichnowsky gave him many opportunities to perform and a great deal of help and encouragement – even suggesting Beethoven live in his own household. But Beethoven was far too much of an individual and, although he remained good friends with the Prince and took him up on his offer for a short time, he preferred to live in his own style.

Perhaps because of his strange, hard childhood, perhaps because he lived largely shut off in a world of music, Beethoven was a difficult man to get along with, prone to take offence and to lose his temper. His teachers, especially, found him incredibly difficult to cope with. He seemed so arrogant, so sure of himself. He believed that greatness lay within him and was irritated by people who did not understand his aims. Beethoven needed their knowledge – but he was certain that he would make his own mark on the world of music.

"Great thoughts float through his [Beethoven's] mind which he can only express through music. Words are not at his command. His whole culture is very neglected and, apart from his art, he is rough but honest and without pretensions. He says straight out what is on his mind. In his youth, and even now, he has had to struggle with disappointments. This has made him suspicious and grim."

Xaver Schnyder, a Swiss composer, in a letter to Hans Georg Nägeli, 1811.

War

In 1794 the French armies of Napoleon swept across Europe and the Elector of Cologne, Beethoven's former employer, was driven out of Bonn. He and many of Beethoven's old friends – Franz Wegeler, Count Waldstein and Stephan von Breuning – settled in Vienna.

Beethoven's brother, Caspar, was already making a living teaching music in Vienna. Now the youngest brother, Johann, arrived and took a job as an assistant to an apothecary. At last, the weight of supporting the family had fallen from Beethoven's shoulders.

In 1795, aged twenty-four, he made his first public appearance – as opposed to the many concerts he had given in court and private homes. His reaction to his audiences could be unnerving. He was known to stand up at the end of a concert, bellowing and exploding with laughter. But the audiences seemed to take it in their stride, putting it down to artistic temperament.

In the same year, he published his Opus 1:

three piano trios. The dogged and exhausting years of study were coming to an end. At long last Beethoven was finding public recognition.

Beethoven's compositions were astonishing everyone in their originality and power. He was an acclaimed pianist. In 1796 he twice went on concert tours in Prague, Dresden, Berlin and Hungary. In Berlin he was presented with a solid gold snuff box crammed with gold coins, of which he was enormously proud.

But all about him the struggle for Europe continued. Napoleon was leading his armies from victory to victory. In 1797 Austria was forced to sign a peace agreement with France. Beethoven, like many of his friends, began to see Napoleon not as an enemy, but as a man setting Europe free from old, narrow ways and bringing with him new freedom and new hopes.

Typhus

In 1797 Beethoven, at the age of twenty-six, was taken dangerously ill with typhus, the name then given to a raging fever accompanied by a wandering of the mind. It was an illness that was to affect his entire life – but the moment he felt well enough he returned to the strenuous round of lessons and concerts and composition. He needed to work at his music – and he needed an income.

Until Beethoven's day all musicians were employed by courts, nobles or religious institutions. Their status was more or less that of a servant. They wrote what they were told to write. But the time had come when someone of Beethoven's gifts could earn a living and fame without being bound to one court or patron. Patronage existed – but without the old demands and restrictions. A gifted artist was now someone who commanded respect – though he still had to tread carefully.

Such changes in the old patronage system, together with the great enthusiasm for music in Vienna, gave Beethoven the opportunities he needed. As a pianist he was the toast of the city. If

This picture shows the surrender by the Austrians to Napoleon after their defeat at the Battle of Austerlitz in December 1805. As a result of this, a very cultured French Ambassador moved into Vienna and, it is said, suggested that Beethoven compose the "Heroic" symphony, in celebration of Napoleon Bonaparte.

he was eccentric and a little unpredictable, it was forgiven for his dazzling performances. But his long apprenticeship, combined with the advent of the new instruments and orchestra, were about to change completely his status in musical history.

First Symphony

It was on April 2, 1800, at the first concert organized entirely for himself, that Beethoven presented his First Symphony to the public. He was twenty-nine.

The critics had been very impressed by the originality of his earlier work and looked for something spectacular in this new venture. But it was fully rooted in the old classical tradition. Beethoven is regarded as the first of the Romantic composers and the last of the Classical, but it did not have the excitement they expected. However, it did contain original ideas and was well received despite the critics' reservations.

Until 1800, Beethoven was seen as a great pianist and a competent composer. Yet all this was to change. One of the first to realize the greatness of which he was capable was his friend and patron, Count Waldstein. This letter wished Beethoven well, as successor to Mozart, when he first left Bonn for Vienna. Beethoven dedicated a Sonata in C to Count Waldstein in 1804.

Beethoven playing for his friends. He was always unwilling to play his own piano compositions in public and preferred to improvise which was a highly-regarded skill. One rival said, "no man . . .has heard extempore playing, unless he has heard Beethoven." However, it was often impossible to get Beethoven to play at all – he was extremely obstinate about playing for people.

For Beethoven the year was a busy one – he published the First Symphony, solo sonata and several shorter pieces for piano, a horn sonata six string quartets, a septet and three concertos. Beethoven himself especially liked the Sonata opus 22.

In addition to this he had been asked, with no previous experience of writing for the stage, to compose music for a ballet named *Prometheus*. It had, over the course of the year, had twenty-three performances, a phenomenal number for the time. Prince Lichnowsky was now paying Beethoven a substantial amount each year, but Beethoven was not completely dependent on Lichnowsky for money, as he was making a living from his compositions, his concerts and his teaching. Still, despite his success, Beethoven was prone to great swings of mood and eccentricity.

Even at concerts in the Lichnowsky house he would "stick his head round the door and make sure there was no one there he disliked" before entering. Other composers would dress elegantly for these occasions while Beethoven "appeared almost ill-dressed, his hair hanging shaggily about his face". He was said to speak with a strong dialect and was considered unmannerly and haughty – in that he would not play the piano if he did not want to.

But Lichnowsky understood him – and treated him like a friend and brother, and saw to it that virtually the whole of the Austrian aristocracy did the same."

However gruff his manner, Beethoven always inspired affection and friendship. Those who knew him knew that his appearance and abruptness hid a warm and loving heart.

The von Brunsviks

Although he was gaining recognition for his compositions and his concert performances, Beethoven continued to teach.

In 1799, two young countesses, Thérèse and Josephine von Brunsvik, had come to Vienna, very excited at being taught by such a master. Beethoven and his pupils enjoyed the lessons and each other's company and soon Beethoven took to staying, not the agreed hour, but all afternoon.

He was delighted by the entire family and they took him to their hearts, just as the von Breunings had. Beside Josephine and Thérèse, their sister Charlotte, their brother Franz and their seventeen-year-old cousin, Countess Guilietta Guicciardi were in the household. Guilietta was also to take piano lessons.

Beethoven became very fond of all the girls – the beautiful Josephine, the delicate Thérèse and the dazzling Guilietta. He spent a great deal of time in their company, both in Vienna and at their country estate in Hungary. Later, Giulietta remembered him as shabby, "very ugly, but noble, sensitive and cultivated".

His shabbiness was so often commented on that it is very easy to forget there are other descriptions of him looking very smart indeed – in

Guilietta Guiccardi – to whom Beethoven dedicated his "Moonlight" Sonata. One of Beethoven's great loves, they were never to marry. There were two main problems in Beethoven's love life. Firstly, he was not of the same social rank as the women he loved and secondly, he could not tear himself away from his music. He could not completely give himself up to the love of a woman despite a strong desire to, so he remained a bachelor.

a blue frock coat with metal buttons and white stockings. Whether shabby or smart, he seems always to have been meticulous in wearing clean linen, in shirt and neckerchief.

As Beethoven's reputation grew, people came to recognize him as he walked the streets of Vienna completely absorbed in composition, his hat rammed onto the back of his head, so that the brim curled, and his pockets bulging with his music notes.

He was a good teacher, even though he grew weary with teaching at times. He expected excellence from his pupils, as he did from himself.

The techniques demanded by the old clavier were quite different to those used in playing the pianoforte. The old staccato striking of the keyboard had to give way to the new subtleties of resonance and expression. The pedals had scarcely ever been touched – now they were an important part of performance. Even the hands had to be held differently – Beethoven taught that the hands be placed on the keyboard so that the fingers did not rise any more than necessary – the way pianists hold them today. Thérèse wrote, "he did not tire of holding down and bending my fingers – which I had been taught to raise and hold flat".

The techniques he passed on to his pupils gave them a range and control that had never previously been dreamed of.

Carl Czerny

One such pupil was a little boy who was taken to see Beethoven as a potential teacher. He and his father went up to Beethoven's rooms and were let in by "a rather grubby servant". It was "a very barren-looking room, papers and clothes strewn all over the place, a few boxes, bare walls, hardly a single chair save the ricketty one by the fortepiano."

There were several people there and the poor child must have been very unnerved by this short, stocky, untidy man with his brilliant blue eyes, his

Opposite: The chaos of Beethoven's rooms. The deafness that grew worse with the years did not, of course, prevent Beethoven hearing the music in his head, in its perfect form. The frustration came in no longer being able to hear and control orchestral performances – or to communicate with other people.

Below: Beethoven wanted expression and power in his music and he introduced dramatic new techniques into playing the new piano to achieve that. He kept the fingers bent so that they were almost covered by the hand. This way he could get more character from the instrument.

deeply scarred, unshaven face and his shaggy black hair. But Beethoven could be very kind.

He gave the boy his full attention, sitting beside him at the ink-stained piano and playing alongside him. The small boy noticed that Beethoven's hands were very hairy and his fingers, especially the tips, were very broad. But the thing that fascinated the boy most was the cotton wool "that had been dipped in some yellow liquid [and] stuffed into Beethoven's ears".

Beethoven was pleased with the boy's playing and took him on as a pupil – teaching him the raised hand position and to use his thumbs. He taught him to use the pedals and to play legato. All new techniques. The boy, Carl Czerny, later became a great pianist in his own right.

Today Beethoven is known as a composer, and the part he played in altering the way people thought about and used the piano is forgotten. His dramatic and powerful way of playing was in complete contrast to the light staccato manner that had been considered correct before. He changed the way people thought about the piano – and transformed piano performance.

Poor and ugly

Of all his pupils, Beethoven had been most dazzled by Guilietta Guicciardi – although she found him fascinating, in later years she remembered him as poor and ugly. And he was both. His face was pock-marked and red. It was once believed he had smallpox when he was young, but doctors today think that the attack of typhus in 1797 may have left him with an arterial disease causing permanent damage to his blood supply.

Certainly, he had once flown into such a rage with a tenor at a rehearsal that he had collapsed and found himself temporarily deaf. It looks as though his damaged arteries could not cope with the high blood pressure brought on by his temper.

Though he was of strong physique, large-boned and muscular, Beethoven had for many years been tormented by recurring bouts of stomach

Above: Just one of Beethoven's many houses in Vienna.
In fact, Beethoven moved about sixty-four times in the
thirty-four years that he spent in Vienna. He was always
being given notice, or giving notice, to leave – he was too
noisy, he spilt too much water on the floor when washing
so that it seeped through to the apartment below, he thought
people were trying to steal his music, there was not enough
sun, people were hanging around outside trying to catch a
glimpse of him. . . . His conversation notebooks are full
of addresses all over the city. He usually rented two or three
apartments at the same time and would live in any one of
them – this made it very hard to visit the esteemed composer!

disorders that sapped his strength and interfered with his work. No one understood such matters then, but this may have affected his body's absorption of vitamins and protein and worsened the arterial trouble.

Now he was suffering more than ever from this recurring illness – but there was a far greater worry. He had begun to notice that his hearing was failing. Beethoven grew more and more anxious. He believed the deafness was somehow linked to his illness and it may well have been – but when the stomach trouble had been successfully treated and his hearing grew steadily worse he became frightened.

He, to whom sound mattered more than anything else, was faced with the prospect of permanent and total silence.

Optimism

Franz Wegeler, Beethoven's friend from Bonn who was now a doctor, had done all he could to help. He advised on specialists and treatments – but by 1801, Beethoven's hearing was far worse. In July, Beethoven told Wegeler that his ears "buzz and hum continually, day and night". He could barely understand quiet conversation, yet someone shouting was an agony. He begged Wegeler to keep his deafness a secret – for fear that people would mock him.

In November Beethoven wrote again, far more cheerfully, "I am now living a more agreeable life in as much as I go out more among my fellow men. You can hardly imagine how dreary and sad my life has been for the last two years. My weak hearing haunted me everywhere, like a ghost and so I avoided people. I must have appeared a misanthrope, though I am far from being one."

And in 1802 he wrote, there is a "lovable charming girl who loves me and whom I love. He even dreamt of marriage, although she was far above him in social rank, a thing that mattered a great deal in those days.

The girl was Guilietta.

"For me there can be no relaxation in human society, no refined conversations, no mutual confidences. I must live quite alone and may creep into society only as often as sheer necessity demands; I must live like an outcast. If I appear in company, I am overcome by a burning anxiety, a fear that I am running the risk of letting people notice my condition."

Ludwig van Beethoven, writing to his brothers in "The Heiligenstadt Testament"

His hopes and happiness were short-lived. There is some confusion about what happened, but they appear to have decided that there was no future possible for them.

They seem to have parted without anger, though some believe it was losing her that played a part in the misery Beethoven felt that summer.

However, in future years he was to tell a friend that the separation was for the best. His whole life was music – there was no room for love and domesticity. For him, music was "the nobler, the better course".

Yet it must have hurt him to give up his dream of marriage. In the summer of 1802 he went, as he had done for the past two years, to spend a few months in the countryside he loved so much. He took lodgings in the town of Heiligenstadt and began work on his second symphony.

But, for once, neither music nor his love of the countryside could drive out Beethoven's fears for the future. He was tormented by the prospect of becoming totally deaf.

The Heiligenstadt Testament

Alone and increasingly depressed, thirty-two-year-old Beethoven sat down in his rented room and made out his Will – and he wrote a long letter to his brothers. It is perhaps the most moving of all his letters – confused, disjointed, awkward, but revealing the darkness through which he was struggling.

It is known as the Heiligenstadt Testament.

It begins with what reads like a cry of anguish. He knew that people thought him obstinate and anti-social, but they had not known the reason. A man who had always enjoyed companionship, he had found himself cut off from everyone by his lack of hearing. He had been "overcome by a burning terror" in company – always afraid they would realize he was deaf.

At one point he had felt he could bear it no longer and thought of suicide. He wrote, "It was only the thought of my art that held me back. It

Beethoven became a familiar sight in the streets of Vienna, striding forward, his hat rammed on the back of his head, completely lost in composition and ignoring everyone around him.

Opposite: Beethoven desperately tried many hearing aids – but none were successful. By the age of forty-eight, normal conversation was impossible. However, he continued to compose. Pictured here is the music for the "Eroica", the symphony in which the spirit of man seems to triumph against all odds.
Below: Beethoven after writing the Heiligenstadt Testament.

seemed impossible to leave the world before I had created all that I felt it was my destiny to create. I decided I must endure my suffering."

"It is hard," he wrote, "for a young man … to behave like a philosopher and accept everything with patience." His letter ends with a cry from the heart, "O providence, give me at least one day of joy. For so long any sense of inner joy has been denied me." He half longed for death – and yet he was determined to live.

His immense courage – the courage of a man who has looked at death and despair and chosen to live and work and create – was to become part of his music.

As a man, Beethoven had many faults, but through his music he makes people believe that there is the possibility of greatness in humanity and that strength and serenity and laughter can survive apparent disaster.

The Second Symphony

Beethoven's growing deafness, however terrifying, did nothing to hinder his work. In the weeks that followed the writing of the Heiligenstadt Testament, he completed the Second Symphony, a work combining calm and radiant beauty with his extraordinary sense of fun. It was a considerable advance on his First Symphony, but, despite its inventiveness, it was still rooted in the earlier musical tradition. Yet a critic saw in it something special – a "spirit of fire".

Like many musicians, Beethoven had "perfect pitch" – the ability to name any note on hearing it. This remained with him when deafness had deprived him of, or distorted, exterior sounds. He could still "hear" music with absolute accuracy in his head – the thought of the pure notes rather than the notes translated by instruments: though from his long experience, he knew the way each instrument would sound them.

He did employ hearing aids and, in the beginning, arrangements to enhance the sound of his piano – but his real composition was done striding

about Vienna – or in his beloved countryside.

His outbursts of temper and violence were probably because some outward event had interrupted his inner perception. In a way his "real" world was inside his head.

The new road

Earlier, in 1801, Beethoven had written, "I am not satisfied with my works up to the present time. From today I mean to take a new road."

He delayed taking this path until 1802 after the Heiligenstadt Testament. It was as if, in facing his deafness and accepting the future, he had gained the courage to put into practice the ideas that had been filling his mind. He had tentatively tried experimental ideas. He wanted to put the traditional ways of composition behind him and create in a far bolder and more original way.

In 1803 he was engaged as resident composer at the *Theater an der Wien*. This *Theater* was the only one in the whole of Vienna to stage German rather than Italian opera.

In April 1803 a benefit concert was arranged for Beethoven – something that he, always short of money, must have been thankful to take part in. However much he earned in his life, handling his finances seems to have defeated him and his affairs were always in a hopeless muddle.

It was a new opportunity to demonstrate the range of his abilities and he chose to attempt the oratorio form and composed "Christ on the Mount of Olives" for chorus and orchestra. It was written incredibly quickly and although it contained some fine music, was very uneven.

The great C major sonata – the *Waldstein,* dedicated to his friend, the Count – was to be his crossing over into unexplored territory – the first step on his "new road".

Beethoven drove himself furiously, reducing himself to a state of complete exhaustion. But by the spring of 1804, his third symphony, the *Eroica,* was complete.

The *Eroica* was to have been his tribute to

Napoleon Bonaparte, but when he heard that Napoleon had crowned himself Emperor, taking the crown from the hands of the Pope, Beethoven was bitterly disappointed. This man whom he had believed to be a great hero was proving to be greedy, proud and self-seeking. He tore up the title page with the words "to celebrate the memory of a great man", and simply named the work, *The Eroica*, the heroic symphony.

It was rehearsed and performed for the first time in the *Theater an der Wein*.

The new era

The symphony bewildered those who heard it for the first time – it was such a completely new concept, so powerful, so much of a unity. It represented a huge step forward, not only in Beethoven's own style, but in the history of music. The first movement is one of the longest ever written and magnificent in its complexity and drama. The two massive chords in E flat that begin it seem simplicity itself, but were not come by easily. Beethoven wrestled with those first few bars for a long time, as his notebooks show. He wanted to declare from the first that this was to be an extraordinary work . . . the beginning of a new era in music.

Almost at once, the cellos descend to C sharp. No classical symphony had ever made such a change so near its start. The second movement begins with a funeral march, a sad and solemn procession. Yet, all through the movement, mourning alternates with moments of something very like defiance, in the blare of trumpets. The final movement, the fourth movement, has been said to show how people, having confronted terror, can still triumph in spirit. And that it is in some ways a portrait of Beethoven himself.

Illness

Beethoven had been obsessed by composition in the years 1803 to 1804. Not only had he written

One of the many portraits of Napoleon as hero. Beethoven, like many people who dreamed of greater freedom in Europe, at first saw Napoleon as a hero. He rid Europe of many injustices and made it possible to rise by talent rather than by influence and ancestry. However, when in 1804 Napoleon crowned himself, many felt he had betrayed the cause of freedom and that power had gone to his head.

the *Eroica,* but the *Waldstein* sonata and much more. He was exhausted, and his normally unpredictable temper was worse. By May 1804, he found himself utterly spent.

Stephan von Breuning saw how wretched he was and took him into his rooms. Almost at once, Ludwig was taken desperately ill – and it was Stephan who nursed him through the crisis, and the fever that followed. Beethoven was so on edge, so suspicious of people's motives, so quick to anger, that it was difficult even to speak to him.

While he had been working he had been able to push his deafness into the background. Now, weak from illness, all his old fears returned – and he lashed out in frustration and misery at the person nearest to him. Stephan. And yet when Stephan wrote to Franz Wegeler, his letter was full of compassion, "You cannot conceive, my dear Wegeler, what an indescribable, I might say fearful, effect the gradual loss of his hearing has had on him."

However, after weeks of tension they had a terrible quarrel and Ludwig, restored to health by Stephan's care, left for the country in a rage.

"Appassionata"

As so often in the past, the calm and beauty of the countryside quietened Beethoven's mind. He was able to concentrate completely on his work and was soon absorbed in composition. He returned to Vienna restored to health and happy again.

The composition was the *Appassionata,* a sonata one critic described as "the eruption of a volcano, splitting the earth asunder and blotting out daylight, while hurtling its missiles into the air!"

Beethoven immediately gave Stephan a little picture of himself with a letter begging him to hide "the memory of all bitterness" behind it. He said he knew how much he had hurt Stephan but that he had been punished for it. He had missed Stephan's company so badly, and had come to realize how important the friendship was and

always would be.

Despite his courage, constant illness, deafness, the pressure of concerts and the enormous strain of composition, made life hard for Beethoven. But, underneath the loving heart was constant. His friends accepted him as he was.

In love

Under intense family pressure, Beethoven's pupil, Josephine von Brunsvik, had married a man far older than herself. It was not a happy marriage. In 1804 her husband died, leaving her with four little children. All through the years of her marriage Beethoven had gone on teaching her and they had become fast friends. Now, in her distress, it was to him she turned for comfort. Gradually, they began to realize that they loved one another. For a year they were happy in each other's company – but the Napoleonic Army was advancing on Vienna and Josephine fled to her country estate in Hungary with the children. When she returned they felt there was no hope of a future together because of the social differences between them. She decided the wisest thing was not to see him again and, deeply unhappy, Beethoven accepted her decision.

Beethoven found comfort in her sister Thérèse, who had long been his friend. Later, in 1846, Thérèse looked back to the days when "this stupendous spirit" had been their friend – and sighed for the fact that Josephine had married someone else. "She would have been happier with him," Thérèse wrote. Josephine had put the security of her children before her own happiness and so had taken as her second husband a wealthy man, instead of Beethoven.

Beethoven and Thérèse were very alike in temperament and interests and over the years their friendship gradually grew into love. It is believed that this was to be the deepest love Beethoven was ever to know.

"Fidelio"

The coming years were to be the most creative of Beethoven's life. During the year 1805, he was completely obsessed by writing his only opera *Fidelio*. By September, it was finished, but there were endless delays and muddles and production had to be postponed until the November. In those few months everything had changed. Vienna had become a city of occupation – Napoleon's army was in possession. A few Viennese and the French military were all the audience for the first three performances.

Fidelio was a failure – not only because of the conditions imposed by war. A great deal needed to be done to give it the form and impact a stage demanded. Beethoven objected to everything that was put forward, but in the end the long suffering Stephan von Breuning pulled it into shape.

In 1806, with a new overture – Leonore 3 – it was re-staged. It was still only a moderate success and made little money. Beethoven must by now have been earning a considerable amount, but his financial affairs were always in a chaotic state and his tendency to suspect people of swindling him led to many arguments.

However, his heart, if not his temper, was, as ever, good. As a mark of their enduring friendship, he wrote Stephan a little song to thank him for his work on *Fidelio* and dedicated his new violin concerto to him.

The Fourth Symphony

It was in this year of 1806 that Beethoven wrote the great Razumovsky string quartets.

Count Razumovsky was an amateur musician who had established a permanent quartet in his household – the first and only example of its kind in Austria. It had become not only the Razumovsky Quartet, but Beethoven's. The players were put entirely at his disposal and it was with them that he worked out some of his finest compositions. At this stage, he had begun work on his Fifth Symphony, but he set it aside and

A scene from "Fidelio", Beethoven's only opera. The story is of the rescue of Florestan, a political prisoner, by his wife, Leonora, who disguises herself as the jailer's male assistant, Fidelio. The Leonora overtures are sometimes played at concerts – but the 4th overture, "Fidelio", is the one used in the opera.

completed the light-hearted Fourth which may well have coincided with his relationship with Thérèse von Brunsvik.

The Fifth Symphony

Once the the Fourth symphony was completed, Beethoven, turned back to the Fifth. It was to change the world of music.

The entire first movement is based on four ominous notes which some have called "Fate knocking at the door". Nothing like it had ever been heard before.

The phrase recurs again and again throughout the work and creates a link between all the movements, an idea that was to be taken up by later composers.

The second movement presents us with a lilting melody that gives way to a march-like theme, and the two alternate and intertwine. We have Beethoven's notes for this movement and we can see the struggle he had before he found what he was looking for.

None of his work came to him easily. He wrote and rewrote, often using notes he had made years before. One composition would feed another. In

This page and inset opposite: In the summer months Beethoven would leave the city for the peace of the countryside surrounding Vienna. Beethoven walked the hills and valleys, weaving the sounds and spirit of nature into his compositions.

he extraordinary surge of creative energy that possessed him during these years, he now embarked upon a sixth symphony.

The "Pastoral"

The summer months of 1807 and 1808 were spent in the country towns of Baden and Heiligenstadt. The Sixth Symphony, the *Pastoral,* was written at Heiligenstadt and was a great outpouring of his love for the countryside. Beethoven did not intend it to be a straightforward description of country scenes – though he gave titles to some passages. He wrote, "Anyone who has the faintest idea of country life will not need many descriptive titles to be able to imagine what the composer meant."

Long after, when he was totally deaf, he was to walk through the valley where he had wandered while composing the *Pastoral.* He asked the friend who was with him if he could hear any yellowhammers in the trees, but all was quiet.

Then he said, "This is where I composed the scene by the stream. The yellowhammers up there and the quail, the nightingales and the cuckoos composed with me."

Astonishing

In December 1808, Beethoven, now thirty-eight appeared at his own benefit concert, at which the Fifth and Sixth Symphonies were performed for the first time, together with his Choral Fantasia The rehearsals for the concert were a shambles and the orchestra at one point declared they would not play at all if Beethoven was in the hall He himself said of the concert, ". . . the musicians were especially angry and, through carelessness made mistakes in the simplest, plainest piece. I suddenly told them to stop, and called out in a loud voice 'Begin again!'. Such a thing had never happened before; and the public were very pleased."

It must have been an overwhelming experience to attend that concert. Beethoven's Fifth made a tremendous impact. The French composer Berlioz, had persuaded his teacher to go and hear it and later met him in the passage. Berlioz began to ask the teacher what he had thought of it but "Ouf!" the man said "I must get out into the air. It is astonishing, wonderful! I was so overcome that when I came to put on my hat I could hardly find my head!"

Absorbed in composition

In 1809 Beethoven had been offered the position of *Kapellmeister,* master of the chapel, at Casse by Napoleon's brother Jerome, whom Napoleon had made King of Westphalia. It was a tempting offer and Beethoven might have accepted it, but his admirers in Vienna did not want him to go. He was, after all, the jewel in the city's crown!

His patrons, Prince Lobkowitz, Prince Kinsky and Archduke Rudolph, offered him an annuity a yearly payment, if he would stay – and he accepted their offer.

Beethoven's increasing deafness and his irascible nature were driving him into senseless and bitter arguments with all about him – including Countess Erdody in whose home he had an apartment, Stephan von Breuning and his friend Ferdinand Ries. He saw intrigue and disloyalty where there was none, he was frustrated by his inability to hear and exhausted by illness and overwork. He could become completely absorbed in composition, wherever he happened to be, and would wander out of eating houses without paying. The proprietors put up with it, partly because they thought him a mad genius – and partly because he had influential friends. These same factors probably saved him from arrest, too, for he was dangerously outspoken in his politics – a liberal and passionate in his belief in freedom.

Love and friendship

Beethoven was working against a dramatic background. In 1809, Napoleon's army once again encircled Vienna. Beethoven, driven almost to desperation by the vibrations of the bombardment, retreated to the cellars, put pillows over his ears and composed Piano Concerto No.5 – the magnificent *Emperor.*

As usual, he was at work on several compositions at once and he dedicated a sonata to Thérèse von Brunsvik. During the years their love story came to its almost inevitable end. A friend wrote that he believed that Beethoven had found he could not face the reality of marriage. Something in him could not give up the life he lived – a life dedicated to music – although he longed for love.

In 1810, Beethoven once again discovered a family that delighted him. The von Breunings, the von Brunsviks and now the Malfattis. Once again, they were musical, cultured, happy and welcoming. "I am so happy with them," he said. They make me forget all the wounds which wicked people have inflicted on my soul." Some of this "wickedness" may have existed only in his

"Beethoven very much enjoyed the company of women, especially those with pretty young faces, and generally, if we happened to see a pretty girl, he would turn around, ogle her pointedly with his eyeglass and laugh or grin when he noticed that I had been watching him. He was frequently in love, but generally not for very long. Once when I chaffed him about his conquest of a beautiful lady, he admitted that she had captivated him more thoroughly and for longer than anyone else – namely for seven whole months."

Ferdinand Ries,
Beethoven's pupil.

47

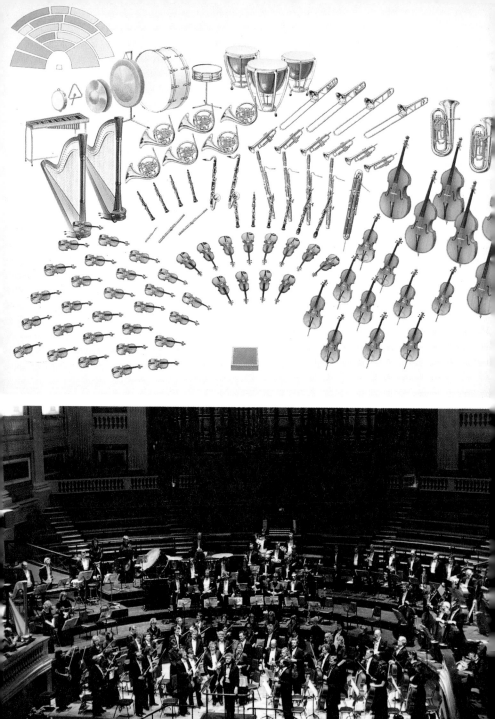

mind but to him the wounds were very real. The Malfatti's dog liked him and followed him about: 'He has eaten beside me in the evening and even accompanied me home. In short, he provides me with very good entertainment."

Laughter again

The elder daughter was nineteen and a fine amateur pianist. Beethoven, in his search for love, decided to ask her, many years his junior, to marry him. Sadly, his proposal was not very well received by the family. The upper classes could admire this genius, this eccentric, ugly, "golden-hearted" man, but it seems that they wanted him neither as husband nor as son-in-law.

A young woman named Bettina Brentano now introduced herself to Beethoven. She was full of life and good spirits, clever and confident. She longed to meet Beethoven, but her friends warned her how difficult and brusque he could be. Perhaps this seemed a challenge to her. Daringly, she called on him without a chaperone, and told him how much she admired his work. Beethoven liked her – maybe she was a good listener – and explained all his feelings about life and music to her, telling her that he felt he was intended to be a channel to bring music to humanity.

Whatever their relationship, she made him laugh again. People were astounded to see this strange couple arrive at a ball, hand in hand. His deafness made conversation with the guests impossible but he took out his notebook and made little entries in it all evening. At the end, he said to Bettina, "My song is finished." He had spent the evening writing it for her, and declared he had read it in her eyes. For so gruff a man, he could be wonderfully charming.

Teplice

1812 was a year of drama. In June, Napoleon's army had invaded Russia, sure of victory, but the Emperor over-extended his lines of supply and

Opposite top and bottom: The form of the orchestra has altered over the years. In the seventeenth century the constitution of ensembles was very flexible indeed. By the eighteenth century, instruments were improving. The whole string family – violin, viola, cello and double bass – replaced viols, wind instruments had arrived and a keyboard was used. By the nineteenth century, the range of instruments was far larger and the sounds had greater range and "character". Composers demanded these new groupings and the increased range of instruments to express their ideas.

the Russian army and the near-Arctic winter defeated him. On the terrible retreat from Moscow starvation, bitter cold and a Russian cavalry that attacked out of the snow and darkness destroyed much of what remained of Napoleon's army. Out of the five hundred thousand who had been engaged in the campaign, fifty thousand survived.

The news swept through Europe. It seemed unbelievable. Change was in the air, bringing with it new hopes and new fears. Now forty-two Beethoven's health was growing worse. In 1811 and now again in 1812 his doctors sent him to the spa town of Teplice for treatment.

In Teplice Beethoven met the great poet novelist, and playwright, Johann Wolfgang von Goethe. Both Bettina and Beethoven admired him greatly and Bettina had longed for the two giants of their age to meet. When the two men did meet, it was not a success. They were too unalike in habit and temperament. Beethoven played for

Beethoven was given a grand piano made by Broadwood that had a special inscription on the sounding board. It accompanied him from house to house as he moved all over Vienna. Although he started his career as a pianist, he stopped playing in public and advised all composers against composing with a piano in the room as it was only a distraction.

the poet, but felt Goethe did not really understand or appreciate his work. They parted on good terms, but never met again.

However, Goethe understood Beethoven better than the composer realized. He told people that he was astounded by the range, intensity and energy of Beethoven's talent – and that he understood very well how his deafness inevitably made him erratic and difficult.

It was at about this time that a deep and mysterious love came into Beethoven's life. After his death, a letter was found in a secret drawer in his desk addressed to "The Immortal Beloved". The entire letter is an outpouring of love and longing, "My angel, my all, my very self.... Love demands all and rightly so, and thus it is for me with you, for you with me...."

No one knows who she was or how Beethoven's relationship with her ended.

The Eighth Symphony

Russia was a long way from Teplice – and yet the war touched everyone's lives. The Austrian government had, because of the war, to devalue its currency. Beethoven's annuity lost more than half its value. The Archduke tried to put things right, but of the three partners in the annuity, Prince Lobkowitz was in financial trouble and Kinsky had died. Beethoven, in a mood of suspicion, thought he was being swindled and threatened his patrons with legal proceedings.... Yet Prince Lobkowitz and Beethoven remained friends. The composer seems to have had an extraordinary ability to make and keep friends, however badly he behaved.

Beethoven's increasing unreasonableness now sent him to Linz, where his brother, Johann was a very successful apothecary living happily with his housekeeper. Beethoven seemed to forget the days of being in charge of his brothers were long past. He ordered the couple to separate and behaved so outrageously the inevitable happened. Johann married the housekeeper.

Bettina Brentano, the vivacious twenty-five-year-old who brought laughter back into Beethoven's life. She was a writer and composer herself and was keen to introduce Beethoven to the poet, Goethe. Although the two did not get on very well, Goethe quickly recognized the special nature of the great composer. "Never before have I seen an artist with more concentration, more energy, more awareness," he said.

It seems impossible that in this atmosphere of squabbling and distrust, Beethoven should have composed a work as fine as the Eighth Symphony.

The Eighth was completed only a few months after his Seventh. Like the Seventh, it looks back to the earlier classical orchestra of Mozart and Haydn. But Beethoven's composition showed that he could create the new "largeness" without using the massive orchestra that was becoming popular, even though the movements are comparatively short and compact. It was not received well – but Beethoven decided that this was because the audience was too stupid to recognize good music when they heard it!

The Panharmonicon

Beethoven was at the height of his creativity – but part of his life about this time was taken up with a very strange business. A friend, Maelzel, was both a musician and an inventor who had been experimenting with ear trumpets to try to help Beethoven's hearing.

Maelzel had invented a mechanical brass band – on the pin and rotating cylinder principle used in musical boxes – and he and Beethoven decided they would make their fortunes by taking this Panharmonicon to England. Beethoven was to write a piece of music, *The Battle*, for the contraption, to give it credibility. This was to celebrate the victory of the Duke of Wellington over Napoleon in Spain in June 1813, a victory which freed Spain from Napoleon's French domination.

To gain publicity and financial backing, Maelzel and Beethoven were to present an orchestrated version of the piece, together with the Seventh Symphony – which was to add depth, at a concert in aid of wounded soldiers.

Beethoven conducts

Though now profoundly deaf, Beethoven wanted very much to conduct the *Battle* Symphony. The orchestra – made up of Vienna's finest musicians –

The metronome, patented in 1814 by Beethoven's friend, J.N. Maelzel, a pianist with an inventive streak. It works by clockwork and enables the tempo of a piece of music to be indicated accurately. A composer writes M.M. (Maelzel's Metronome) at the head of the composition and then numbers to show the number of crochets to the minute. Beethoven's initial reaction was, "It is silly stuff, one must feel the tempo", but some of his music is marked with M.M.

was very nervous and their fears were justified.

Beethoven conducted with his entire body: in the softer passages he sank almost to his knees and was hidden behind the conductor's stand and as the music grew in force, he would reach up until he was on tiptoe, his arms flailing.

But he could not hear. Gradually, he gained on the orchestra. In the end the *Kapellmeister* quietly motioned to the musicians, stood behind Beethoven, and conducted from there.

The piece was a resounding success. Vienna loved the histrionics of the so-called *Battle Symphony*. It far outstripped the Seventh in popularity and acclaim, for anti-Napoleonic feeling was at its height.

But Maelzel, Beethoven's partner in the Panharmonicon scheme, had legal rights to the original tune and now tried to get them for the orchestrated version. He had copies made behind Beethoven's back and produced the piece in Munich. So Beethoven took him to court. The legal battle dragged on for four years until 1817, when, after much waste of time, money and energy, the two men made up their differences and agreed to share the costs.

Yet, this obstinate, quarrelsome man could be both perceptive and kind. A baroness had lost her only child. She was numb with grief, unable to cry or speak about her loss to anyone. Beethoven asked her to his home and said quietly, "Now we will talk in music" and played to her for over an hour. At last the tears came. She remembered later, "He said everything to me [in his music] and gave me consolation at last."

Guardianship

By 1815 Beethoven seemed to be prospering financially – but his younger brother, Casper, had developed tuberculosis, the same dreadful sickness that had killed their mother. Beethoven helped the family with money and, when Casper died, accepted the guardianship of his son, using most of his money to secure the boy's future.

Casper had stipulated that nine-year-old Karl should stay with his mother but Beethoven without wife or child of his own, took over the lad and sent him away to school. He thought Karl's mother "a bad woman" and did all he could to keep them apart. Karl, caught in the middle tried to keep the peace – and learned to lie.

By 1817, the forty-seven-year-old Beethoven was extremely deaf and could hear nothing of music and he could no longer hear voices. His ever-faithful friend, Ries, tried to persuade Beethoven to accept an invitation to write two symphonies for the Philharmonic Society of London – and to travel to England. But he was now totally immersed in a long and complex sonata, the "Hammerklavier".

The greatest living composer

Against a background of difficulties with Karl Beethoven embarked in 1819 upon a Mass, the *Missa Solemnis,* intended for the enthronement

of Archduke Rudolph as Archbishop.

It took Beethoven four years of intense concentration – and was finished long after the ceremony had taken place. At the same time, he had been working on the Ninth Symphony – the *Choral* – and on three piano sonatas.

To make some money, Beethoven entered upon a piece of underhand dealing, by promising the exclusive rights of the Mass to several different people. In money matters he could be both careless and untrustworthy.

In 1822, *Fidelio* was revived and Beethoven tried to control the rehearsals, even though he was now totally deaf. The orchestra struggled on for some time, but eventually a note was handed to Beethoven, telling him to go home. He left the building in utter despair.

At only fifty-two, Beethoven was now regarded throughout Europe as the greatest living composer. As such, celebrities flocked to visit him and were astonished at the kindliness of their hero. He was generous in praise, encouraging and interested to learn about their work.

The Ninth Symphony

Vienna, always fickle, was now in love with the sparkling music of Rossini, but when Beethoven at last finished the Ninth Symphony and threatened to give its first performance in Berlin there was a hasty petition to have it presented in Vienna. It was performed there in 1824.

The symphony seemed to sum up everything Beethoven had experienced and believed in all his life. Through it he seemed to speak of the predicament of humankind – bewildered, uncertain, overwhelmed by forces greater than itself. And yet, at the last, he declared that this is only part of the whole – and that the gift of life is a supremely joyful thing.

At its end, the audience were clamorous in their applause – but it was only when the young contralto took Beethoven's arm and turned him to face them that he could see the ovation.

Karl, now nineteen, was at university, but Beethoven was pushing him far too hard. The young man wanted to join the army, but his uncle would not allow it. His only concession was in letting him transfer to a commercial college.

Beethoven was obsessed by Karl and could never leave him in peace, deluging him with letters of advice and reproach to distraction. In the end, Karl could stand it no more. In July 1826, he drove into the countryside and shot himself.

Mercifully, Karl lived but Beethoven was in turmoil. Karl told the police that he had done it because his uncle "tormented him too much". As a result, Stephan von Breuning generously took over Karl's guardianship and got him accepted as a cadet in a good regiment.

Karl and Beethoven went to stay at the country estate of Beethoven's brother, Johann, until the boy was well again. There was an uneasy truce between them and Beethoven began work on what was to be his last string quartet.

Failing health

But Beethoven was not at all well and Johann very wisely decided it was imperative that Karl join his regiment. In spite of his failing health, Beethoven felt duty bound to see his nephew safely to Vienna.

There was no closed carriage available and so, on December 1, 1826, they set off in an open one. The weather was bad, and the journey wretched. Beethoven, already in poor health, developed a cough, and by the time they reached Vienna it had turned to pneumonia.

A doctor was sent for at once and his prompt treatment seemed to avert any danger. Certainly, Beethoven felt well enough to write to the Wegelers as cheerfully as usual. Karl, who was going through the preliminaries before joining his regiment, came to see him every day and he seemed well on the road to recovery.

But a few days later he suddenly became very ill. Dr. Malfatti was sent for – uncle to the girl

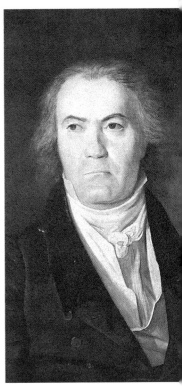

A portrait of Beethoven in 1823 by Ferdinand Georg Waldmuller. Beethoven's chronicler, Schindler, declares it to be "further from the truth than any other". Yet Waldmuller was the greatest artist ever to paint the composer. Another writer declares that at least it shows Beethoven as he "growls and scowls" and conforms to the romantic, tragic hero image of the composer.

Twenty thousand people attended Beethoven's funeral – it took one and a half hours for the cortège to cover the five hundred paces to the church.

Beethoven had once wanted to marry. But while his treatment helped, it soon became obvious that the improvement had only been temporary. Beethoven had developed dropsy and jaundice and was in extreme pain.

Friends and admirers came to visit him. Though

edridden, he greeted them all with affection and
ook a great interest in their affairs. He talked –
hrough his notebooks – of politics and the state
f the arts in Vienna, read the proofs of the
Choral Symphony – and talked of a tenth. Yet he
lso spoke with sad regret of the home and family

The statue of Beethoven outside his birthplace in Bonn. In remembering Beethoven's work, we must remember the cost: the long struggle against hardship, ill health and isolation. But we must also remember that in all his suffering, he rejoiced in life, the beauty of nature and the excitement of creativity.

he had never had. He had so much love to give – but music demanded all his heart and mind and left no room for marriage.

A young soprano sang for Beethoven who, despite his deafness, delighted in her expression. He took enormous pleasure in discovering the songs of Schubert. An old friend remembered how he yearned for the complete works of Handel and sent all forty volumes.

The end

But his illness was beyond all cure. The doctor recognized that death was very near and sadly wrote his conclusions on Beethoven's notepad. Beethoven read the words calmly, as if with complete acceptance. He had very little strength left, but with quiet determination made his Will, leaving everything to Karl. He received the priest with gratitude and courtesy – and lay back on his pillows.

On March 24, 1827, Beethoven slipped into a coma. Two days later, on March 26, the sky was overcast, snow swirling in a bitter wind. At about four the sky grew darker and a snow storm buffeted the windows. Suddenly there was a great clap of thunder and a flash of lightning that lit up the room. It seemed to rouse the dying man. Those watching beside the bed saw him open his eyes, raise his right hand with fist clenched – and then lay it down upon the bed again.

The battle was over. Ludwig van Beethoven was dead. He was only fifty-six – yet he had left a legacy of music that altered the path of classical composition. He reached out to the hearts of the people of his own time and to ours.

Twenty thousand people attended his funeral on March 29 – and mourned him not only as a great musician but as a friend. His heart and his music had been filled with a longing for freedom and with a belief in the dignity of humanity and its courage in the face of every trial.

Out of his own suffering he created a most incredible beauty.

Important Dates:

770 Dec 16: Ludwig van Beethoven is born to Maria and Johann van Beethoven, in Bonn, Germany.

778 Johann takes eight-year-old Ludwig touring. He makes his first appearance as a keyboard prodigy in Cologne.

780 Ludwig begins to learn to play the organ at a local monastery with Friar Willibald Koch.

781 Ludwig begins lessons with Christian Gottlob Neefe.

782 Neefe leaves eleven-year-old Ludwig to deputize for him as Court Organist.
Nine of Ludwig's piano variations are published by Neefe.
Ludwig begins to deputize for the *Kappellmeister* in leading the court orchestra.

784 Beethoven, aged fourteen, is given his first salaried post as Court Organist.

787 Beethoven raises enough money to travel to Vienna where he receives keyboard lessons from Wolfgang Amadeus Mozart.
July 17: Ludwig's mother, Maria van Beethoven, dies of tuberculosis.
Ludwig returns to Bonn.

789 Beethoven is made one of the viola players in the *Theater* orchestra and is given the post of chamber musician.

792 Nov 2: Beethoven leaves Bonn for Vienna. He begins lessons with the composer, Haydn.
Dec 18: Beethoven's father, Johann, dies.
Beethoven begins lessons with Schenk, without Haydn's knowledge.

794 Beethoven begins lessons with the musical theorist, Albrechtsberger.

795 Napoleon's army sweeps across Europe.
Opus 1 – three piano trios – is published.

796 Beethoven tours Prague, Dresden and Berlin.

797 Beethoven falls ill with typhus, but returns to work as quickly as possible.

799 Beethoven begins teaching keyboard skills to the von Brunsvik family and Guilietta Guicciardi.

800 Apr 2: The first concert entirely arranged for Beethoven takes place and he presents the First Symphony.
Beethoven composes music for the ballet, *Prometheus*.
Beethoven realizes his hearing is deteriorating, but wants to keep it a secret.

802 Oct 6/10: Beethoven, aged thirty-two, writes the "Heiligenstadt Testament".
He composes the Second Symphony.

803 At a benefit concert arranged for Beethoven, he introduces "Christ on the Mount of Olives".
The *Waldstein* is Beethoven's first step on his "new road".

1804   The *Theater an der Wien* is the venue for the first performance of the Third Symphony, the *Eroica*.
Beethoven then falls ill and returns to the country to recover.

1805   The *Appassionata* is published.
Beethoven falls in love with Josephine von Brunsvik, but the relationship comes to an end when she leaves for the country.

1806   Nov: Beethoven's only opera, *Fidelio,* is produced.
Beethoven composes the Razumovsky Quartets, as well as the Fourth Symphony. This coincides with his relationship with Thérèse von Brunsvik.

1808   The Fifth Symphony is completed as is the Sixth Symphony, the *Pastoral*. Both are presented, along with the *Choral Fantasia,* at a benefit concert.

1809   Prince Lobkowitz, Prince Kinsky and Archduke Rudolph decide to pay Beethoven an annuity after he is tempted by an offer of *Kappellmeister* out of Vienna.
Piano Concerto No.5, the *Emperor*, is completed.

1810   May: Forty-year-old Beethoven asks the nineteen-year-old Malfatti daughter to marry him. He is rejected.
Bettina Brentano introduces herself to Beethoven and the two become friends.

1812   Napoleon invades Russia and is defeated.
Beethoven spends the summer at Teplice where he meets the poet, Johann Wolfgang von Goethe. He also writes, but does not send, a letter to "The Immortal Beloved".
He composes the Eighth Symphony.

1813   Between them, Beethoven and Maelzel, an inventor, devize a money-making scheme involving the Panharmonican. Beethoven composes the *Battle* Symphony for the machine. They begin a four-year legal battle over the rights to the music.

1815   Beethoven's brother, Caspar, dies of tuberculosis and Beethoven becomes guardian of his nine-year-old son, Karl. Beethoven immediately removes the boy from his mother and sends him to school.

1817   Beethoven's deafness worsens and he can no longer hear voices.

1819   Beethoven works on the *Missa Solemnis* for the enthronement of Archduke Rudolph as Archbishop.

1823   Beethoven finishes the *Missa Solemnis* and works on the Ninth Symphony and three piano concertos.

1825   Beethoven's nephew, Karl, goes into the countryside and shoots himself. He survives and he and Beethoven spend time together while Karl recovers.

1826   Returning to Vienna with Karl, Beethoven contracts pneumonia.

1827   Mar 26: Ludwig van Beethoven, aged fifty-six, dies.
Mar 29: Twenty thousand people attend Beethoven's funeral.

Musical terms

Chamber music: Music written for a small group of solo musicians and originally intended to be played in a small room.

Choral fantasia: A fantasia is a piece of music which is composed in a more free and imaginative fashion than usual. Beethoven's *opus* 80, is a "fantasia for chorus, *piano* and *orchestra*".

Classical tradition: The musical style that was popular between about 1750 and 1810. The characteristics of this type of music are elegance and grace of melody, with clear form and balanced textures.

Clavier: Any type of keyboard.

Concerto: A type of composition in which a solo instrument contrasts and "competes" with an *orchestra*. It usually has three *movements,* and the soloist is given difficult and showy passages to play. Beethoven wrote several – his most famous is the "Emperor" concerto.

Contralto: The lowest female voice. Occasionally, a high male voice is used.

Counterpoint: This is a type of texture in which two or more melodies are woven together.

Improvisation: Music which is performed as it is composed. It is rarely written down and many of the improvisations of Mozart and Beethoven have been totally lost.

Legato: A musical term which means "smoothly".

Major key: Music based on certain notes which form a major scale. Major keys tend to sound brighter than minor keys.

Mass: The form of worship of the Roman-Catholic Church. The five main sections can be sung, usually in Latin and sometimes with orchestral accompaniment.

Minor key: Music based on certain notes which form a minor scale. The first movement of Beethoven's "Moonlight" *Sonata* is in a minor key.

Movement: A single piece of music which is put together with other pieces or movements, to make a larger form.

Opera: A play which is entirely sung. The characters are performed by vocal soloists and accompanied by *orchestra.*

Opus: This means "work". Opus 1 means the first work of a composer.

Oratorio: Similar to an *opera,* but the subjects are always religious. Today, the oratorio is not acted, it is performed as a concert.

Orchestra: A large combination of instruments which plays together as a group. It is usually divided into four sections – woodwind, brass, percussion and strings. Beethoven's orchestra was quite small when he started to compose. Later in his career, he made the orchestra larger and used some unusual instruments.

Overture: An orchestral piece in a single *movement.* During Beethoven's lifetime the overture was written as an introduction to an *opera* or *oratorio.* Later overtures were written as entirely separate pieces of music.

Pianoforte: A keyboard instrument invented by Cristofori in 1698. He named it pianoforte, which translates as "soft-loud", as this was the first instrument which could easily play both by using hammers to hit the strings. Now known as the "piano".

Piano trio: An ensemble of players – *piano,* violin and cello. The name refers to the players and the music.

Quartet: Music for four voices or four instruments.

Quintet: Music for five voices or instruments. A *piano* quintet is a string *quartet* plus *piano.*

Romantic tradition: The musical style that was popular between about 1810 and 1900. The music was often emotional and dramatic, using freer forms than those used by *classical* composers. The *orchestra* was larger, and new instruments were developed. Composers were very interested in the other arts, and stories, poems or pictures were used to base music around.

Score: A master-copy of a piece of music showing all the parts of each instrument. The instruments are always written in the same order down the page. The players themselves read from orchestral parts showing only their own music.

Sonata: This word has two meanings. Firstly, a composition for solo *piano* or solo instrument accompanied by a *piano.* Secondly, a type of form popular in the *classical* period. Most *symphonies* had at least one *movement* in sonata form.

Soprano: The highest female voice.

Staccato: A musical term meaning short or detached.

Symphony: A large *orchestral* composition, usually in four *movements.*

Tenor: A high male voice.

Viola: A string instrument – slightly larger and deeper than the violin.

Recommended listening

Piano Sonata No.14. "Moonlight" Sonata: Beethoven wrote this in 1801 when he realized that he was becoming deaf. The first movement is slow which is unusual – most sonatas start fast. The music reminded a critic of moonlight reflecting on Lake Lucerne in Switzerland. From then, the piece has been nicknamed the "Moonlight" Sonata.

Razumovsky String Quartet No.1: This was written for four players said to be the finest in Europe. Count Razumovsky played 2nd violin. As a tribute to the Count, Beethoven used a traditional Russian melody in the finale of this work.

Piano Concerto in E No.5 ("Emperor"): This was Beethoven's last piano concerto. The music is very dramatic, but also very delicate.

Symphony No.5: This is probably the best known of all Beethoven's works.

Mass in D major (*Missa Solemnis*): This belongs to the last period in Beethoven's life when he became totally deaf. The piece reflects the depth of Beethoven's religious beliefs despite the fact that he was never a member of any church.

Index